D1671566

MYTHOLOGY OF THE WORLD

MONSTERS AND CREATURES OF WORLD MYTHOLOGY

by Clara MacCarald

BrightPoint Press

San Diego, CA

© 2023 BrightPoint Press
an imprint of ReferencePoint Press, Inc.
Printed in the United States

For more information, contact:
BrightPoint Press
PO Box 27779
San Diego, CA 92198
www.BrightPointPress.com

LIBRARY OF CONGRESS CATALOGING-IN-PUBLICATION DATA

Names: MacCarald, Clara, 1979- author.
Title: Monsters and creatures of world mythology / by Clara MacCarald.
Description: San Diego, CA: BrightPoint, [2023] | Series: Mythology of the world |
    Includes bibliographical references and index. | Audience: Grades 7-9
Identifiers: LCCN 2022039974 (print) | LCCN 2022039975 (eBook) |
    ISBN 9781678204983 (hardcover) | ISBN 9781678204990 (pdf)
Subjects: LCSH: Monsters--Juvenile literature. | Animals, Mythical--Juvenile literature.
Classification: LCC GR825 .M147 2023 (print) | LCC GR825 (eBook) |
    DDC 001.944--dc23/eng/20220912
LC record available at https://lccn.loc.gov/2022039974
LC eBook record available at https://lccn.loc.gov/2022039975

CONTENTS

AT A GLANCE

- Mythologies from cultures around the world include a variety of monsters and creatures.

- Monsters such as the Sumerian Humbaba and the Greek Hydra battled with mythical heroes.

- Fenrir the wolf and the Midgard serpent fought with the Norse gods. Both would kill important gods at the end of time.

- Dragons could be wise and helpful, as in Chinese mythology. Other dragons were fierce monsters.

- Mythical horses included the flying horse Pegasus from Greek mythology and the eight-legged horse Sleipnir from Norse mythology.

- Other mythical creatures included Greek centaurs and satyrs. In Roman mythology, fauns were similar to satyrs.

- In Chinese mythology, foxes tricked people to steal their energy. Kelpies from Scotland were water monsters who ate people.

- The Chinese god Pangu and Ymir from Norse mythology were giants who helped create the world.

- Mythic folk included the Tuatha Dé Danann, who were fairies from Celtic stories, and little helpers called Aluxo'ob from Maya mythology.

INTRODUCTION

THE DRAGON'S TREASURE

One day, the Norse gods Odin, Loki, and Hoenir killed an otter. But the otter wasn't really an animal. It was a dwarf **shapeshifter**. The shapeshifter's father was Hreidmar (HREYD-mahr). Hreidmar became furious at the gods. He forced them to give him a huge pile of treasure as

payment for his son's death.

Hreidmar's son Fafnir became greedy.

Fafnir killed his father so he could take the

Hreidmar's son spent his days fishing as an otter.
He returned to his father and brothers each night
as a dwarf with all the fish he had caught.

Sigurd was able to kill the shapeshifting dragon Fafnir. But before Fafnir died, he passed a terrible curse onto Sigurd.

riches for himself. He hid the treasure in

a cave. He then turned into a dragon to

protect it.

Fafnir's brother Regin also wanted the treasure. He convinced the hero Sigurd to challenge the dragon. Sigurd found a path from the cave that led to a watering hole. He dug holes under the path. He then hid in one and waited. When the dragon passed overhead, the hero thrust his spear into Fafnir's heart.

When Fafnir asked for Sigurd's name, Sigurd answered without hesitation. He did not realize the power this word offered the dying beast. It enabled Fafnir to pass a curse onto Sigurd. The curse would later lead to Sigurd's death.

MONSTERS AND CREATURES IN MYTHS

Monsters and fanciful creatures are found in myths from all around the world. Monsters gave form to people's greatest fears. They also pushed the limits of what people could imagine. Some creatures were enormous. For instance, the Midgard **serpent** of Norse myth circled the entire world. Some creatures had amazing features. A monster could have a hundred heads. It could have the body parts of many different animals.

Monsters were often a threat that a hero had to overcome. But not all monsters were

The Midgard serpent wasn't always so big. He grew to his enormous size after Odin threw him into the sea.

bad. Some creatures gave aid to heroes

or other mythical characters. Still, it was a

good idea not to cross the creatures.

1

FEARSOME FOES

Many great hero stories include a terrifying monster. The need to slay a monster gave a hero an exciting goal. The hero could display enormous courage by facing the monster.

GUARDIAN OF THE CEDAR FOREST

Gilgamesh was a mythical king in

Mesopotamia. Mesopotamia was a region

in the Middle East. Gilgamesh hoped to

make himself and his friend Enkidu famous.

He decided they would rid the world of

Humbaba. This giant monster guarded the

Many heroes in myths have a goal of slaying a monster. Winning a battle against an evil monster can be a symbol of good defeating evil.

Cedar Forest. The creature had lion's paws tipped with the claws of vultures. Horns topped his head, and his tail ended in a snake head.

The *Epic of Gilgamesh* was a piece of ancient writing that told the story of the two heroes. In the **epic**, Enkidu was afraid of Humbaba. He told Gilgamesh, "His speech is fire and his breath is death."[1]

But Gilgamesh would not listen. Enkidu gave in. The heroes traveled to the monster's home. There, Gilgamesh and Humbaba fought. Their struggle kicked up a terrible storm. The heroes and the monster

The Epic of Gilgamesh describes Gilgamesh and Enkidu as looking almost identical. Even many experts have a hard time telling the heroes apart in ancient carvings.

split Cedar Mountain in half. Finally, the sun god blinded Humbaba so Gilgamesh could capture him. Humbaba begged for mercy. But Enkidu struck off his head anyway.

FOES OF THE GREEK HEROES

Several monsters battled Greek heroes. One such beast was the Chimera (ki-MER-uh). She was a fire-breathing **hybrid**. The Chimera was a lion in front, a goat in the middle, and a dragon in the rear. In some images, she has a snake as a tail.

The hero Bellerophon set out to slay the Chimera. On his way, he tamed the flying horse Pegasus. Together, Bellerophon and Pegasus attacked the monster. But Bellerophon's arrows were not enough to kill her. Bellerophon forced a lump of lead down the Chimera's throat. The beast's own

The National Archaeological Museum in Italy has a bronze Chimera statue on display. It shows the hybrid animal with a snake for its tail.

flames melted the lead. The liquid choked

her to death.

Another terrible monster was the Hydra.

It was like a giant water snake with many

heads. The Hydra killed men with its

poisonous breath. If someone chopped one

The hydra had one immortal head. But Herakles found a way to keep the monster from hurting anyone again.

head off, two grew back. One of the Hydra's

heads was immortal.

The hero Herakles hunted the Hydra

with his nephew Iolaos (eye-oh-LAY-ahs).

Each time Herakles cut off one head, Iolaos

burned the stump. Doing so stopped that head from growing back. The hero buried the immortal head. He put a heavy rock on top to keep it underground.

FOES OF THE NORSE GODS

In Norse mythology, the god Loki had **monstrous** children whom the gods feared. One was Jormungand. This huge snake was also called the Midgard serpent. The god Odin tossed the serpent into the sea. In the 1200s, poet Snorri Sturluson told stories from Norse myths in his book the *Prose Edda*. He wrote that the Midgard serpent "lies in the midst of the ocean, surrounds all the earth, and bites his own tail."[2]

The Midgard serpent was Thor's enemy. Thor was the Norse god of thunder. Once, he went fishing for the Midgard serpent. He used an ox head for bait. The great serpent took a bite. Thor tried to pull the monster

MYTHOLOGY AND MARVEL

In 2017, Marvel Studios released the movie *Thor: Ragnarok*. The Marvel Universe made changes to the characters. The movie turned Fenrir into Fenris. Fenris is female. In mythology, Hel is Fenrir's sister. She is a monster who rules the dead. In the movie Hel is Hela. She is Thor's sister. Hela raises Fenris from the dead to fight at Ragnarok.

into his boat as it sprayed poison at him. A

giant who was with Thor became terrified

and cut the line. The Midgard serpent

got away.

Loki's son Fenrir was an enormous wolf.

The gods decided to trick him to keep

themselves safe. They challenged him to

break free from different kinds of ropes.

They hoped to keep him tied up. But Fenrir

was too strong.

The gods asked the dwarves to make

a magic cord. The dwarves spun the cord

from the roots of mountains, bird spit, and

other unusual objects. But Fenrir didn't

Fenrir was unlike other wolves. He was enormous, with strength to match his size.

trust the gods this time. The god Týr put his hand in Fenrir's mouth to prove to the wolf the gods weren't trying to fool him. When Fenrir realized he couldn't break free, the wolf bit off Týr's hand in a rage.

Norse mythology says both the Midgard serpent and Fenrir will face the gods when

A MONSTER FAMILY TREE

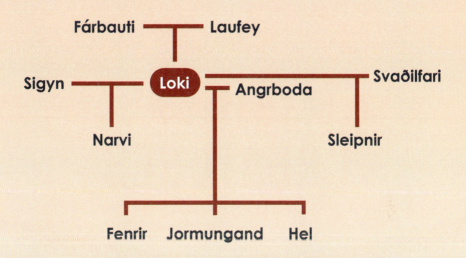

The Norse god Loki was the son of a giant and the parent of monsters.

the world ends. The end time is known as Ragnarok. The Midgard serpent will rise from the sea. Thor will kill the serpent before dying from its poison. Fenrir will eat Odin. Odin's son Vidar will slay the giant wolf in return.

2

MYTHICAL CREATURES

Many famous monsters come from myths. Dragons played several parts in different stories. In addition, some creatures, such as the flying horse Pegasus, became well known. But the eight-legged horse Sleipnir (SLAY-p-neer) was much less so.

DRAGONS OF THE WORLD

Dragons came in different forms depending on the myth. Most appeared similar to a serpent or lizard. Some had wings or many heads.

There were many kinds of dragons in Chinese myths. Some had human heads.

Odin's horse Sleipnir had magical powers. He could travel over land or sea or even fly through the air.

Others had animal parts, such as a horse head or tiger paws. Chinese dragons could have scales, horns, or a magic pearl below their jaw.

Some Chinese dragons flew through the sky. Their breath formed clouds, and they could control the rain. Most were powerful, wise, and helpful. Some were **divine**.

Yinglong was a dragon god. He helped the hero Huang Di fight Chiyou. Chiyou was a flying monster with horns, hooves, four eyes, and six hands.

Yinglong took away all the water from Chiyou's territory. This made it so Chiyou

Some Chinese dragons were said to live in the oceans. They protected sailors.

and his army had no water to drink. Huang

Di then managed to catch Chiyou.

The Egyptian monster Apophis who

tried to stop the sunrise is sometimes

called a dragon. Apophis was the Great

Serpent whose roar echoed through the

underworld. His gaze could bewitch the gods themselves.

MONSTERS OF THE UNDERWORLD

The monster Ammut lived in the Egyptian underworld. *The Complete Gods and Goddesses of Ancient Egypt* was written in 2003. The book talks about Ammut. "Her head was that of the crocodile, her neck, mane, and foreparts those of the lion . . . and her rear quarters were those of the hippopotamus."[3]

Ancient Egyptians believed that when people died, their souls appeared in the

Ammut was an odd-looking creature. She had the body parts of a crocodile, a lion, and a hippopotamus.

Hall of Truth. The god Osiris judged each

soul. He weighed the person's heart against

a white feather. The feather represented

harmony. If the heart outweighed the

feather, the person was judged as wicked.

The number of heads that Cerberus had depended on the myth. Even with just three heads, the creature looked incredibly fierce.

Osiris would then give the heart to Ammut to eat. The soul would disappear instead of moving on to the afterlife.

The monster dog Cerberus guarded the Greek underworld. In early myths he had one hundred heads. In later stories about

Cerberus, he usually had three. The heads of snakes rose from his back. He also had a snake as a tail.

Cerberus kept the living out of the underworld. He acted friendly toward the dead if they behaved. Cerberus ate anyone he caught trying to leave.

Some of the living heroes got the better of the fierce guard dog. Herakles wrestled Cerberus and hauled him out of the underworld. In Roman mythology, the hero Aeneas (ih-NEE-uhs) passed the monster with the help of a **prophet**. She drugged Cerberus so he fell asleep.

Bellerophon tamed Pegasus. But the mythical horse ended up serving Zeus.

In Maya myth, the vision serpent connected the living and the dead. Royal Maya burned blood as an offering for the gods. The blood could be their own or from someone they killed. The offering was said to make the vision serpent appear. Gods and dead people could then talk through the serpent to the one performing the ritual.

MYTHICAL HORSES

Medusa was a monster in Greek mythology. She had snakes for hair. The flying horse Pegasus was her son. He was born from Medusa's blood after the hero Perseus cut off Medusa's head and killed her.

One day, the hero Bellerophon grew too confident. He tried to ride Pegasus to Mount Olympus. This was the home of the Greek gods. Zeus grew angry that Bellerophon dared to approach the gods as an equal. Zeus sent a fly to bite Pegasus. The startled horse flung the hero off. From then on, Pegasus served Zeus.

In Norse mythology, the eight-legged horse Sleipnir was Loki's son. However, Loki was not Sleipnir's father. Loki was his mother. Loki was in the form of a mare when he gave birth to the creature.

Sleipnir became Odin's faithful horse. In many stories Sleipnir was huge. His hoofprint could create a canyon. In other versions he was the size of a regular horse.

But he was always magical. His many legs
let him reach great speeds.

Norse mythology states that Sleipnir will
ride into battle with Odin during Ragnarok.
The horse will help fight Loki and Loki's
other children. After Odin and Sleipnir die,
Sleipnir will carry the god into the afterlife.

THE SLIDING ONE

The word *Sleipnir* meant "the sliding one" in Old
Norse. The magical horse Sleipnir may have been
named this because he could move swiftly between
all nine realms in Norse mythology. He could even
travel to the realm of the dead and back.

3

PART HUMANS

Mythical creatures could be part human. Some were animal hybrids. Some had human heads or bodies as well as animal parts. Other part-human creatures were shapeshifters. They could use their powers to trick people.

OUT OF EGYPT

The Egyptian sphinx was a symbol, not a monster. Images of the sphinx appeared more than 4,400 years ago. The sphinx was a lion with the head of another animal.

Most people could not solve the Sphinx's riddles. But Oedipus saved the city of Thebes when he answered her correctly.

Some sphinxes had human heads. A sphinx statue could represent a king or a sun god. The image of the sphinx spread from Egypt into Asia and Greece.

The Sphinx of Greek myth was a monster that haunted the city of Thebes. She asked a riddle of anyone coming to or leaving the city. When people could not answer the riddle, she ate them.

The Sphinx asked Oedipus (EH-duh-pus) what had four legs, then two, and then three. The hero said that humans crawl on arms and legs as babies. They later walk on two legs. And they walk with a staff when

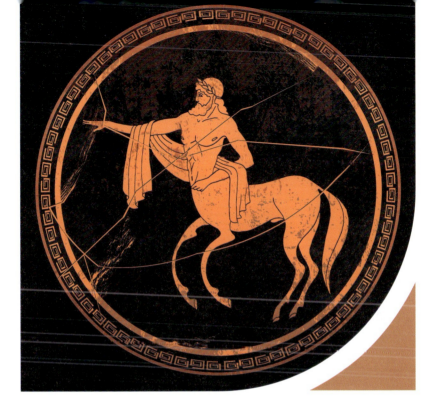

Centaurs were hybrids from Greek mythology. They were human from the waist up with a horse's body and legs.

they are very old. Defeated, the Sphinx

threw herself off a cliff.

OTHER HYBRIDS OF MYTHOLOGY

Centaurs were human-horse hybrids from

Greek mythology. They were human from

Chiron was different from most other centaurs. He helped others with his knowledge from the gods.

the waist up. But they had a horse body

with four horse legs.

Most centaurs were known for drinking

and fighting. Chiron (KI-ron) was different.

In some stories he was the son of the god

Kronos. Other gods taught Chiron arts and medicine. He became the teacher of the heroes Jason and Achilles. He also lost his life to a hero.

Herakles was visiting with the centaur Pholos. A group of other centaurs showed up. They began drinking. Things got out of hand. When the centaurs attacked Herakles, Herakles shot and killed Chiron with a poisoned arrow accidentally.

In the first century CE, the Roman poet Ovid wrote stories of Greek and Roman myths. Ovid told a different version of how the poisoned arrow killed Chiron.

The centaur was visiting with Hercules, the Roman version of Herakles. Chiron examined Hercules's arrows. "And while the old man fingered the shafts clotted with poison, one of the arrows fell out of the quiver and stuck in his left foot," wrote Ovid.[4]

SATYR PLAYS

Ancient Greek theater had satyr plays. The actors dressed in satyr costumes and performed between the acts of other plays. The satyr characters sang and danced as they made fun of the tragedies in the more serious plays. This added humor for audiences.

Satyrs started out in myths as human-horse hybrids like centaurs. Unlike centaurs, they had only two legs. Over time, satyrs became half goat instead. They roamed the woodlands. They were wild and often drunk. They were followers of Dionysus, the god of wine.

In Roman mythology, fauns were similar to satyrs. Fauns also followed Dionysus, as well as the god Faunus. Faunus was the Roman god of the woodlands. He protected shepherds and hunters.

SHAPESHIFTERS

Foxes were shapeshifters in Chinese mythology. In order to shift, a fox had to find a human skull that perfectly fit its head. Leaves and petals became the fox's clothes. As the fox got older, it grew more tails. The oldest foxes could have nine. Foxes also gained knowledge and magical powers with age. There is a collection of Chinese stories written around 300 CE, possibly by a man named Guo Pu. "When they are a thousand years old," the writer says of foxes, "they can commune with the heavens and become heavenly foxes."[5]

Foxes were shapeshifters in Chinese mythology.
The oldest of these creatures often had nine tails.

Kelpies often took the form of horses that tempted people to ride them. The shapeshifting creatures would then drag the humans underwater to their death.

The shapeshifting foxes could suck life energy from people. They could do this without killing the people. The foxes sometimes did good deeds with the energy, such as curing the sick.

The kelpies from Scottish stories were deadly shapeshifters. Kelpies haunted rivers and streams. Often a kelpie looked like a horse. Sometimes kelpies took the form of little blue men or handsome young people.

Kelpies caused lots of trouble. They could make rivers and streams deadly to sail or walk across. As horses, kelpies liked to tempt people to take a ride. They especially liked children. Once humans got on the monster's back, they couldn't get off. The kelpie dragged them underwater to eat them.

4

MYTHICAL FOLK

Many mythologies included mythical races. Some were giants with super strength. Some were closer to the size of humans. These included elves and dwarves. Others were small folk who did their best to hide from people.

GIANTS

Giants are found in many myths. In Chinese mythology, the **chaos** before the world existed became a heavenly egg. The egg held the giant Pangu. He grew to separate the heavens from the earth. When Pangu died, his body formed the world.

In Norse mythology, dwarves were magical creatures. Like elves, many dwarves had a talent for making precious objects.

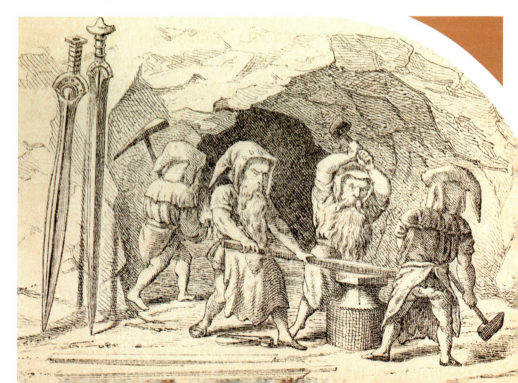

In Norse mythology, the giant Ymir (EE-meer) appeared at the beginning of time at the place where fire met ice. Ymir had children, including the frost giants. Ymir's giant cow licked the ice for three days. It melted and freed a man inside. The man had a son. The son had three gods for children. One was Odin. The gods murdered Ymir. They used his body to form the world.

The Greek hero Odysseus had to outwit a giant with one eye. This was the cyclops Polyphemus (pah-luh-FEE-muhs). Odysseus was traveling with his ship's crew.

A cyclops's single eye gave the giant an even more unusual appearance. Odysseus was almost eaten by one of these enormous creatures.

Polyphemus trapped Odysseus and his crew in a cave to eat them. But Odysseus gave the cyclops wine. It put Polyphemus to sleep. The hero and his men stabbed the monster's eye out. In the morning, they hid under the cyclops' sheep. The blinded monster felt only the tops of the sheep as he let the animals out. The men were able

to escape.

FAIRY FOLK

The Tuatha Dé Danann (THOO-a DAY

DU-non) were an immortal fairy race from

Celtic mythology. They rode into Ireland and

fought a brutal war against the Fomorians,

FROM FAFNIR TO SMAUG

The author J.R.R. Tolkien loved reading myths as a child. He also studied mythology as an adult. His interest inspired him to write *The Hobbit* and *The Lord of the Rings* books. Tolkien filled his stories with dwarves and elves, similar to those in Norse myths. His scenes with a dragon even echoed Fafnir's encounter with Sigurd.

a race of giants. A monster named Balor led the Fomorians. A 2019 article in the *Irish Times* states, "[Balor] had an evil eye in the centre of his forehead which, when opened, wrought destruction all around." The Tuatha Dé Danann ended up destroying their enemies.[6]

After 3,000 years, humans called the Milesians (muh-LEE-zhuhns) arrived in Ireland. The Milesians beat the Tuatha Dé Danann in a war. The Tuatha Dé Danann became fairies and retreated into fairyland. They lived in beautiful palaces. Sometimes the fairies crept into the human world to

Dwarves created Thor's magical hammer Mjöllnir. The weapon was strong enough to help the thunder god fight giants.

take things. They also stole people away to fairyland.

Norse mythology included stories about elves and dwarves. Some elves lived in the heavens. Dwarves often lived underground. A 2021 article on the online *World History Encyclopedia* says, "Elves . . . and dwarves . . . have in common their talent for creating precious objects."[7]

Many stories include dwarves making great treasures. The dwarves made Thor's hammer, Mjöllnir (MEE-ahl-neer). But these mythical dwarves were often greedy and quick to curse people to protect treasure.

BROWNIES AND ALUXO'OB

Brownies were small beings from Celtic myths. They often helped humans, but they stayed mostly out of sight. These creatures cleaned and did chores. Their clothes were shabby and brown. Some people left

In Celtic mythology, brownies helped people with household chores. But sometimes they made mischief by moving people's belongings.

milk for brownies. But if they offered new clothes, brownies would get upset. These creatures were proud of their outfits. They would disappear if humans tried to change them. Treating brownies poorly could turn them into boggarts. Boggarts made messes and broke things.

The Aluxo'ob from the Americas were similar to brownies. They were magical folk the size of young children. Farmers put out food or other gifts for them. In return, the Aluxo'ob helped the farmers. The creatures protected the fields. But they could also scare dogs or make people sick.

Monster myths have been popular for a very long time. Today, people continue to tell stories of mythical monsters and creatures. The creatures show up in modern books and movies, inspiring new stories to entertain and terrify new generations.

GLOSSARY

chaos
disorder and confusion

divine
having to do with gods or goddesses

epic
a long story or poem telling the deeds of heroes

hybrid
a creature that combines two or more kinds of animals

monstrous
being ugly or frightening like a monster

prophet
a person who passes information from a god to other people

serpent
a snake

shapeshifter
a being that can change its form at will

SOURCE NOTES

CHAPTER ONE: FEARSOME FOES

1. Andrew George, trans., "The Epic of Gilgamesh: The Babylonian Epic Poem and Other Texts in Akkadian and Sumerian," *SOAS University of London*, n.d. https://eprints.soas.ac.uk.

2. Rasmus B. Anderson, trans., "The Younger Edda," *Project Gutenberg*, July 31, 2006. www.gutenberg.org.

CHAPTER TWO: MYTHICAL CREATURES

3. Richard H. Wilkinson, *The Complete Gods and Goddesses of Ancient Egypt*. London: Thames and Hudson, 2017, p. 218.

CHAPTER THREE: PART HUMANS

4. James G. Frazer, trans.,"Fasti, Book 5," *Theoi Project*, n.d. www.theoi.com.

5. Rania Huntington, *Alien Kind: Foxes and Late Imperial Chinese Narrative*. Cambridge, MA: Harvard University Press, 2003, p. 1.

CHAPTER FOUR: MYTHICAL FOLK

6. Éanna Ó Caollaí, "Oh God! How Many of Ireland's Deities Can You Name?" *Irish Times*, August 2, 2019. www.irishtimes.com.

7. Irina-Maria Manea, "Elves & Dwarves in Norse Mythology," *World History Encyclopedia*, March 8, 2021. www.worldhistory.org.

FOR FURTHER RESEARCH

BOOKS

S.A. Caldwell, *The Magnificent Book of Dragons*. San Francisco, CA:
     Weldon Owen, 2021.

Stephen Krensky, *The Book of Mythical Beasts and Magical Creatures*.
     New York: DK Publishing, 2020.

Gail Radley, *Fairies*. Mankato, MN: Black Rabbit Books, 2023.

INTERNET SOURCES

"5 Terrifying Tales from Greek Mythology," *National Geographic Kids*, n.d.
     www.natgeokids.com.

"Tall Stories: Were Giants Real?" *DK Find Out!* May 10, 2017,
     www.dkfindout.com.

"Where Do Dragons Live?" *Wonderopolis*, n.d. https://wonderopolis.org.

WEBSITES

Museum of Monsters, Myths, and Legends
www.museumofmythology.com

The Museum of Monsters, Myths, and Legends website includes pages on Greek, Norse, and Egyptian mythology.

Norse Mythology
https://mythopedia.com/topics/norse-mythology

This website explores Norse myths and gods. It discusses the writings that record Norse beliefs as well as how Norse people saw the world.

Primary History KS2: Ancient Greece
www.bbc.co.uk/teach/school-radio/ks2-ancient-greece/zk73nrd

This site from the BBC has links to audio clips and transcripts telling several Greek myths, including ones featuring monsters.

INDEX

IMAGE CREDITS

ABOUT THE AUTHOR

Clara MacCarald is a freelance writer who has written more than forty nonfiction books for kids. She lives with her daughter and a small herd of cats in an off-grid house nestled in the forests of central New York.